Nikki

A Journey of Resilience

Harman Cherra

Dedication

In loving remembrance of my mother, Nikki, an exceptional maternal figure and a beacon of unyielding resilience.

This book serves as a heartfelt tribute to the exceptional journey and invincible spirit she possessed. Her battle with ovarian cancer was characterized by bravery and dignity, confronting each day with a determination that inspired everyone privileged enough to know her.

Mom, you were a steadfast beacon of love, resilience, and support. Your journey demonstrated extraordinary courage in the face of formidable adversity. Your radiant smile and infectious laughter infused our lives with warmth and joy, consistently reminding us of the intrinsic beauty and preciousness of every moment.

Your courageous struggle against cancer attested to your unwavering spirit. You embraced each day with unrelenting optimism, refusing to let the illness define you. Your perpetual faith, resilience, and positive outlook on life deeply touched the hearts of all who knew you.

This book is an offering to your memory, celebrating the legacy of an incredible woman who illuminated our understanding of love, courage, and perseverance. Your endless love and dedication to our family will be forever etched in our hearts, guiding us throughout our lives.

Through the stories told in these pages, we honor your life, highlighting the moments that underscored your extraordinary nature. Your selfless love, limitless kindness, and ironclad resolve continue to inspire us. Your memory lives on, spurring us to meet life's trials with the same strength and grace you embodied.

For those who are facing life's struggles, this book symbolizes hope and resilience. It reminds us that even in the darkest times, we possess the power to prevail, cherish each day, and find solace in our sweet memories.

Mother, while your physical presence may have faded, your spirit persists vibrantly in our hearts and cherished memories. Your legacy of love and bravery continues to guide us, molding our lives with the principles you ingrained within us.

This book is devoted to you, Mother, a true heroine who embodies love, fortitude, and grace. May your spirit continue to glow brightly, illuminating our paths and inspiring us to lead our lives with purpose and fervor.

Acknowledgment

Writing this book has been a deeply personal journey that couldn't have been embarked upon without the support, patience, and encouragement of some extraordinary people in my life.

Firstly, I would like to express my profound gratitude to my son, Jaiden. Your sparkling eyes, unwavering faith in me, and innocent cheerfulness have been my beacon of hope, even in the most challenging moments of writing this book. Your laughter is my favorite symphony, and your hugs are my safe haven. Thank you, Jaiden, for being my most cherished source of inspiration and strength.

I would like to thank my family for their unwavering support. To my father, Dave, thank you for your love, patience, and steadfast belief in my journey. You've always been there for me, and your encouragement has been instrumental in completing this book.

I am deeply thankful for the presence of my sister, Priti, who was with me at every step of this journey. Her insights and memories have added richness to this narrative, and her continued support was invaluable in bringing this book to life.

I am grateful to my friends who have stood by me, offering their help in numerous ways. Your unwavering support, understanding, and encouragement have been invaluable.

I want to thank all the healthcare professionals who were there for my mother throughout her battle against ovarian cancer. Your dedication, compassion, and commitment to your work have left an indelible mark on our family.

I would also like to extend my gratitude to my mentors, colleagues, and everyone in the academic and healthcare community who have enriched my professional journey and personal growth. Your guidance, support, and friendship have been invaluable.

Finally, I want to thank the readers for embracing this book. By engaging with my mother's story, you honor her life and contribute to keeping her memory alive.

This book stands as a testament to the spirit of resilience, love, and unwavering faith. It's a journey of an ordinary woman who left an extraordinary impact on the lives she touched. This narrative would not have come together without the contributions of so many individuals, and for that, I am profoundly grateful.

About the Author

Harman Cherra is a devoted father and compassionate healthcare professional who finds inspiration in the remarkable life of his mother, Nikki. Balancing his career in healthcare with his passion for storytelling, Harman brings a unique perspective to his writing. Through his words, he aims to inspire others to embrace the joys of parenthood and the transformative power of love.

In this deeply personal book, Harman weaves together the narratives that define his mother's life — a legacy of boundless love, remarkable resilience, and unwavering strength. As a source of perpetual inspiration, Nikki's story serves as a testament to the indomitable human spirit.

When not immersed in his professional responsibilities or at the writing desk, Harman finds solace in spending quality time with his family, especially his son, Jaiden. He enjoys exploring the world through travel, cooking traditional Indian meals, and expressing his artistic flair through dance.

Through sharing his mother's story, Harman invites readers to embark on an extraordinary journey, drawing courage from the indelible legacy of an everyday woman.

He hopes that readers will discover the power of resilience through his words and find inspiration in the triumphs and challenges that shape our lives.

Preface

Every life is a tapestry of stories woven together by threads of experiences, moments, and relationships. The beauty of this tapestry often lies hidden in the ordinary, as it is within the everyday moments that the extraordinary reveals itself. This book, therefore, isn't just the story of my mother, Nikki; it is a collection of stories, memories, life lessons, and the love that she embodied.

Writing this book has been an intensely personal journey for me. It was born from a desire to pay tribute to the woman who shaped my world, nurtured my growth, and left an indelible impact on my life. As her son, I had the privilege of knowing her intimately, of witnessing her strength, her resilience, and her unwavering love.

Yet, this book is not solely a tribute. It is also an exploration and a celebration of the principles Nikki lived by. Principles of perseverance, faith, and boundless love. It's about the lessons she taught us, not by her words but by her actions. Lessons about resilience in the face of adversity, about giving selflessly, and about cherishing the beauty of every single moment.

This book also presents the raw and unvarnished truth about life's challenges and tribulations. Nikki faced many obstacles in her journey, from a humble beginning to her courageous battle with ovarian cancer. But through it all, she remained undaunted, her spirit indomitable.

As you journey through these pages, you'll discover the woman who was Nikki. You'll glimpse her laughter, tears, dreams, and fears. You'll walk with her on her journey, sharing her triumphs and trials. You'll get to know the woman who was my mother, mentor, and hero.

This book is my humble attempt to share Nikki's story with the world. But more than that, it's my way of keeping her memory alive, of preserving her spirit. It is a testament to her legacy, one of love, courage, and an unwavering zest for life.

As you read this book, my hope is that Nikki's story will touch your heart, inspire you, and maybe even prompt you to reflect upon the tapestry of your own life. And I hope that you, too, will come to see the extraordinary in the ordinary, just as Nikki did.

I invite you to immerse yourself in this journey, to experience the joy, sorrow, love, and resilience that defined Nikki's life. And above all, I hope her story will encourage you to embrace every moment of your own journey, living life with courage, love, and an unwavering spirit of hope.

Contents

Chapter 1: The Boundless Beauty of Motherhood

"God could not be everywhere, and therefore, He made mothers."

– Rudyard Kipling

The connection between a mother and her child is an extraordinary tapestry of love and devotion, a relationship that transcends words and resonates deeply within our hearts. From the dawn of time, mothers have held a sacred role, providing care, guidance, and unconditional love to their children.

In this chapter, we will explore the profound significance of motherhood, the immeasurable impact mothers have on their children's lives, and the evolving nature of motherhood in our modern society.

At the core of motherhood lies selflessness that knows no bounds. A mother's love is an unwavering force fueled by a genuine desire to nurture and protect her offspring. Whether it is a human, animal, or even a bird, a mother's dedication and sacrifice know no limits. Her instinctual drive to provide the best for her children propels her to brave the storm, conquer mountains, and overcome any obstacle that may come her way. A mother's love knows no bounds, extending far beyond her own needs and desires.

The bond between a mother and her child is a tapestry woven with threads of love, trust, and unwavering support. While both parents play significant roles in a child's life, a mother's connection with her child often holds a unique depth and intensity. From the very moment of birth, a mother is consumed by an overwhelming sense of devotion, dedicating herself wholeheartedly to her child's well-being. Her love is a steadfast beacon, guiding her child through life's triumphs and tribulations.

From infancy through adulthood, a mother's nurturing touch shapes her child's growth and development. In the early stages, she selflessly tends to every need, providing sustenance, warmth, and protection. As her child grows, a mother's role expands, encompassing emotional support, guidance, and a constant source of strength. Her prayers are interwoven with every breath, silently wishing for her child's happiness, success, and fulfillment.

Yet, the true beauty of motherhood shines brightest in the small, everyday gestures. From a comforting embrace during a moment of sadness to a soothing lullaby that lulls a restless child to sleep, a mother's presence is a balm for the soul. She is a source of solid love, a steady hand guiding her child through the twists and turns of life. A mother's joy radiates from her smile, her laughter filling the air with warmth and tenderness. Her unwavering support and belief in her child's potential become the foundation upon which dreams are built.

Across cultures, religions, and generations, the significance of a mother's love remains unshakeable. Her presence is celebrated and cherished as a precious gift bestowed upon humanity. Mothers are the architects of society, shaping the hearts and minds of future generations. Their love knows no boundaries, and their impact reaches far beyond the confines of the home.

In this chapter, we celebrate the enduring love and boundless beauty of motherhood. We recognize the profound role mothers play in shaping lives, fostering growth, and nurturing the seeds of greatness within their children. It is through their selfless love and relentless dedication that they leave an indelible mark on the world, illuminating the path toward a brighter and more compassionate future.

"A mother is she who can take the place of all others but whose place no one else can take."

– **Cardinal Mermillod**

Chapter 2: A Journey Begins

As I tell the story of my mother, Nikki, I am filled with deep admiration and respect for the struggles her family endured. The hardships they suffered and the sacrifices they made are etched deeply into the fabric of her upbringing, stretching back to her parents.

To understand Nikki's family background, we must journey back in time before she was born. Her family hails from the region of Punjab in India, which was occupied by the East India Company during the period of direct British rule over the Indian subcontinent from 1858 until 1947 when it gained independence and split into India and Pakistan. This era was known as the "British Raj."

For Nikki's family, the struggle for Indian independence was of concern, especially given the diverse set of communities living in Punjab. The tensions came to a head in 1947 when the subcontinent was partitioned, and the province of Punjab was divided into East Punjab and West Punjab.

During this tumultuous time, Nikki's parents - Dewan Singh and Charan Kaur - faced unimaginable challenges and were forced to migrate. They bravely led the family to safety, leaving everything they knew behind to start over in present-day India. The journey was treacherous, spanning over a month to travel just 25 miles to a small town called Simbli.

With nothing but clothes on their back, the journey seemed never to end. They witnessed countless atrocities and danger at every turn. It was no less than a miracle that they made it to their new home safely and were determined, more than ever, to start over.

Nikki's father, my grandfather, often narrated stories of their migration and the obstacles they had to deal with just to merely survive. From religion to life, everything was at stake for the first few years after the partition. The volatility of the situation had everyone remaining on the edge. He once shared his account of rescuing the Sikh holy book, Sri Guru Granth Sahib, from a burning temple holding it on his head during their escape. The opposition nearly killed the family, but he fought relentlessly for his rights and the holy book he carried with him. Nikki's boldness came from her father, who himself was a pillar of strength and passion, and meeting him and hearing his stories was an honor that left a lasting impact on me.

Throughout her life, Nikki intently listened to the stories narrated by her parents and learned valuable lessons about the importance of family, community, hard work, and determination to overcome adversity. Her parents instilled in her a deep sense of hope, courage, and perseverance that stayed with her until the end.

Nikki was born in 1958 in Simbli, India, the fourth of six children in a family characterized by hard work, unity, and a deep-rooted belief in the value of education. From an early age, Nikki observed her parents' dedication to the family and their unyielding commitment to building a better future. As she grew older, she absorbed the lessons of resilience, compassion, and perseverance from her father, Dewan Singh.

The life of a farming family in rural Punjab was far from easy. Before Nikki could attend school, she and her sisters were tasked with laborious chores on the family farm. They planted crops, peeled sugarcane, and tended to the cows, enduring long work hours in the early morning. Having worked since an early age, these responsibilities instilled in Nikki a strong work ethic and taught her the importance of contributing to the family's well-being.

Despite the demanding nature of her daily routine, Nikki's commitment to her studies never wavered. She effectively juggled between work and academics and displayed a natural inclination for the latter. While her peers and siblings openly discussed exams and their performance, Nikki remained humble, often downplaying her achievements. But time and time again, she proved herself to be a high achiever, surpassing expectations and shining academically.

Nikki's pursuit of knowledge was not confined to the classroom. After school, she would return to her chores, assisting her family until the day's work was done. In the limited moments of respite, she would study alongside her sisters, determined to make the most of her education and young blood.

Her upbringing in a family of resilience and hard work laid the foundation for Nikki's own determination and perseverance. These formative experiences forged her character, instilling within her an unwavering spirit and a sense of purpose that would guide her throughout her life.

As Nikki entered her teenage years, her family discovered the promise of a new land—the United States of America. Historically, many Punjabi farmers and skilled workers had migrated to North America, seeking better opportunities for themselves and their families. With the passage of the Immigration and Naturalization Act of 1965, which aimed to reunite immigrant families and attract skilled labor, Nikki's family saw a chance to build a brighter future in the land of dreams. It was an attractive prospect with a proven success record for others in their community.

With hope in their hearts and a sense of adventure, Nikki's family embarked on another transformative journey leaving behind Nikki for now. They had left their familiar surroundings; they set their sights on California, where extended family members had already laid down roots. It was a voyage that would retest their resilience, but they faced the unknown with determination and the belief that they could shape their destiny.

The migration to America marked a new chapter in the family's lives—a chapter filled with infinite possibilities, unfamiliar customs, and the challenges of assimilation. But like all others, Nikki embraced this new chapter with the same tenacity and grit that had carried her family through countless trials before. Education remained at the forefront of her ambitions, as she recognized the power it held when finding doors and opening them to achieve success.

As Nikki's story unfolds, we witness the remarkable resilience of a family that refused to be defined by their circumstances. From the throes of twice migration to the toil of daily chores, their journey is one of steadfast faith, unity, and a firm commitment to creating a better future. And at the heart of it, all is Nikki—a young girl whose early years shaped her into a woman of extraordinary strength, compassion, and an unyielding spirit that would inspire all those who crossed her path.

In the chapters that lie ahead, we will explore the transformative experiences that awaited Nikki and her family as they navigated the complexities of a new country and the trials of life. It is a story of hope, resilience, and the enduring power of the human spirit—an invitation to witness the extraordinary journey of a woman who would leave an indelible mark on the lives of those around her and the world at large.

Chapter 3: Embracing New Horizons

"The beautiful journey of today can only begin when we learn to let go of yesterday."

-Dr. Steve Maraboli

There's always an indescribable feeling that envelops you when you stand at the precipice of a new journey in life toward something unknown. Whether transitioning from school to college, embarking on the path of marriage, or venturing into a foreign land to start anew, each experience holds the power to shape your identity and influence the person you become. For Nikki, that moment came when she left India in 1974 at the tender age of sixteen to join her family in the United States of America.

A whirlwind of emotions surged within Nikki as she prepared for this momentous leap. Nervousness and excitement intertwined, creating a mélange of sentiments she couldn't quite decipher. Stepping into an uncertain future, brimming with its own set of challenges and obstacles, is a daunting task for anyone moving to a foreign land. It requires immense courage and resilience to leave behind the familiar, bid farewell to loved ones, and embrace the unknown.

Nikki and her family weren't merely physically uprooting themselves from their homeland; they were also detaching from the emotional connections they had nurtured in India all their life. They had to embrace a fresh perspective, adapting to a new environment that awaited them. They were going to experience a drastic shift from the culture they originally belonged - a vibrant, cohesive, and traditional culture. At the same time, they would see life and live around people who are not scarred by the struggles and atrocities at the hands of the colonizer. Altering one's mindset toward something intangible takes time and effort. The prospect of exploring oneself in an entirely different setting evokes both trepidation and exhilaration. The unknown lies ahead, and all one can do is hope for the best.

As the journey unfolds and you take that leap of faith, you begin to realize the deep-rooted ties you hold with your culture back home. Changing the lens through which you view the world is a gradual process. Yet, therein lies the beauty of trusting your instincts, relinquishing doubt, and welcoming life with open arms. When you possess the foresight to see the bigger picture, you can navigate life's challenges without succumbing to unhealthy temptations, standing resolutely in the face of adversity. So, despite the hesitance, Nikki forged ahead toward her new life.

As Nikki sat in the car on her way to New Delhi Airport, a wave of inexplicable emotions washed over her. The road ahead stretched like dried spaghetti, captivating her gaze until it merged with the distant gray and blue horizon. With little expectations and only fragmented information about her new life, she embarked on this voyage. During her eight-hour drive from her village in Punjab, Nikki found herself contemplating the chapters of her life that had already passed and the adventures that awaited her. She had no idea where this road would lead or even if it would treat her kindly. Now was the time to take control of her emotions, exhibit resilience, and embrace faith.

Life, as we know it, is a tapestry woven from our plans and the unforeseen circumstances that shape our destiny. It's about internalizing our emotions, cultivating an open and growth-oriented mindset, and not allowing circumstances to overpower us.

Constantly glancing out of the car window, she felt the cool breeze, reminiscent of her village in Punjab, caress her face. She closed her eyes, and a tear gently trickled down her cheek. One can never forget the land that witnessed their childhood and adolescence, the foundation upon which their life was built.

This ride was a whirlwind of anxiety, excitement, and uncertainty. Nikki had no inkling of what lay ahead. Grasping the emotional rollercoaster was crucial at that moment. Memories of her neighborhood friends, whom she relied upon and cherished, tugged at her heart throughout the drive.

The thought of not being around them was heart-wrenching, yet the curiosity and eagerness to explore the new life ahead stirred within her. She couldn't envision what lay beyond, but she stood ready to embrace it with open arms.

Upon arriving at the airport, Nikki found it difficult to step in and board her flight. She didn't know when or if she would return or if her homeland would remain the same in her eyes. Memories flashed through her mind, evoking a bittersweet emotion. Leaving behind the country where she had spent sixteen formative years meant bidding farewell to the person she had become amidst all the obstacles. She would have spent a little more while reminiscing her life in India, but time was ticking, and she had to board her flight to the U.S. to embark on a journey that could prove transformative or present unforeseen challenges. Though she had resolved to look ahead, she knew a part of herself would remain behind.

Staring absently through the small oval window, she watched the runway elapse and the plane took off. In the same state of mind, she experienced fluffy white clouds drifting out of sight. With each fading cloud, she whispered to herself that perhaps things weren't as daunting as they seemed and brighter possibilities awaited her on the other side of the globe. The almost day-long flight went past in no time as Nikki was busy recollecting her memories and cherishing them. She often looked around and glanced at the faces of others around the plane, wondering what their stories were. In the same state of mind, she was about to touch the land of the United States of America.

As the plane was descending, she raised her head for a clearer view from the airplane window. Nikki's breath caught in her throat at the sight of the city. It was a breathtaking tableau, with lights breathing life into the landscape like scattered glitter as far as her eyes could reach. The flight was landing, and soon she would step into an entirely new city, ready to embark on a fresh chapter of her life.

Nikki walked toward the sign that proudly proclaimed "WELCOME TO SAN FRANCISCO," her luggage trailing behind her. She slid her passport through the small opening, and the attendant inspected her face with a scanner-like precision. Nikki felt a twinge of discomfort but sighed with relief once the customs process was over. It seemed unnecessary to her, but at least it was done.

On the other side awaited her future, her fortune, and her new life. Strangely, as Nikki ventured further, she felt a newfound sense of freedom and freshness with each breath she took. She approached the next, and an unfamiliar sensation washed over her. The sun illuminated her surroundings from the clear glass, and she drank in the vibrant scenery of the arrival terminal of the airport.

A familiar voice broke Nikki's reverie. "Oye puttar!" her father exclaimed, waving from the crowd gathered along with her mother behind a metal barrier at the arrival gate. A wave of warmth flooded Nikki's chest as she hurried toward them, enveloping her father's broad frame in a tender embrace, then her mother's. It was the most comforting she had felt in the past few days leading up to the flight. Seeing them filled her with an indescribable warmth and a sense of belonging. Regardless of feeling alienated and disoriented on her journey, those emotions dissipated within seconds. They quickly exited the airport, and it marked the first day for the rest of Nikki's life.

The city embraced the urban aesthetic she had only read about in novels. Towering skyscrapers loomed above her while cars weaved through the streets amidst traffic lights. The buildings formed a grid-like pattern, showcasing the organized nature of the city. Amidst the hustle and bustle, people confidently navigated their way, shouting over the noise of cars or walking steadily on the sidewalks.

The city transformed before her eyes as she glanced out of the car window, with downtown areas transitioning from opulent affluence to pockets of poverty. Elite establishments, adorned with fancy lettering and fragrant atmospheres, gave way to rundown pawn shops, dingy supermarkets, and bustling public marketplaces.

Nikki's journey to Yuba City proved to be an exotic one. She found herself caught between trying to make sense of her new surroundings and yearning for a touch of home. Having her family there to welcome her eased the doubts and uncertainty she had been grappling with. She couldn't help but compare the place she cherished the most with this strange world she had entered. Punjab had a continuous symphony of people talking, dishes clattering, and children laughing. Here, however, silence deafened her. The unprecedented cleanliness and organization stood in stark contrast to what she was accustomed to. Glancing at the map of her new house in Yuba City, she couldn't help but find the name peculiar.

The city's scent was foreign, with an overpowering mix of chaos and perfumes that pushed Nikki to her limits. The earthy aroma she was familiar with was absent from the air, overpowered by fumes emitted by vehicles. This feeling of overwhelmingness made Nikki long to see greenery, a sight of Mother Nature that she had already started yearning for. As if her prayers were answered, Nikki spotted fruit orchards in the distance, colors of nature meeting her eyes. She hadn't expected to encounter such expanses of agriculture in this urban landscape, and the sight filled her heart with joy. The lush green fields stretched like a comforting brown, green, and gold quilt. Her gaze then fell upon never-ending rice fields and vegetable farms, evoking a strong sense of nostalgia. This reassured her that even in this foreign land, reminders of home and grounding were within reach. The mere thought uplifted her spirits as she eagerly awaited her arrival in Yuba City.

As Nikki further settled into Yuba City, she gradually began to grasp the concept of the 'American Dream.' She felt a mix of fear and excitement. While in India, Nikki had heard a lot about the 'American Dream' – the ideal notion that the government protects every person's interest and thinks for their welfare. According to this concept, everyone has the right to dream and pursue their own idea of happiness. It suggests that regardless of the social class or societal status one is born into, equal opportunities exist for economic and professional growth. Under this concept, success is achieved through risk-taking, hard work, and sacrifice rather than relying on chance.

This idea inspired Nikki to research and explore how she could progress as a woman in this country. However, she soon realized that the reality was far from what she had imagined. Nikki was well aware that life in the new Yuba City would be a struggle, with the need to work hard to make ends meet and help her family establish a foundation for success in this new world.

In Yuba City, everyone was trying to find their own path, working through their insecurities, weaknesses, and leveraging their strengths to make the best of their lives. Nikki understood that life wasn't as easy as it seemed, and she had to strike a balance between carrying out household duties and earning a living. She knew she couldn't simply abandon her household responsibilities to focus solely on making money. She approached them with a strong sense of self and character, leaving no stone unturned to ensure her family didn't suffer in any way. Nikki realized that with hard work, people of her skin tone could succeed, and her courage gave her the strength to be vocal in a male-dominated family, fearlessly sharing her opinions. She envisioned her family achieving success in farming and frequently discussed growing their family empire with her parents, brothers, and sisters.

With this vision in mind, Nikki and her siblings worked tirelessly, day and night, saving every penny to help their father establish a farming empire. They woke up early, even before sunrise, to prepare food for the long and laborious day ahead. Then, they head to the orchards to work as farm laborers, picking fruits and vegetables. The family's dream was to achieve a comfortable living, but they were well aware that the journey wouldn't be easy.

The entire family got to work early and braved the scorching heat to be dropped off at nearby farms. Nikki often found herself crawling on her hands and knees for hours on end, earning only a few bucks. They had to wear long-sleeve clothes to protect themselves from insect bites. Despite the physical strain, she persisted, knowing that this collective effort would contribute to the growth of her father's farming legacy from Punjab. Her strength and courage became an inspiration for her entire family.

Can you imagine the harsh conditions Nikki had to endure while working? The labor involved in such inhumane conditions required immense willpower and inner resilience to get through each day. Nikki not only fulfilled her duties but also recognized the importance of personal growth through education. Despite managing her family and work, she enrolled in high school with the firm intention of improving her family's circumstances. She understood that succumbing to overwhelming situations would only drag her down, so she focused on personal development and growth. This allowed her to maintain healthy relationships with her family and enhance her overall quality of life.

Personal development and growth is a transformative process that uplifts individuals emotionally, spiritually, socially, and intellectually, leading to a healthier and more productive life. When faced with challenging situations, it empowers individuals to tap into their potential and see satisfying results in both their personal and professional lives. It enhances self-image, self-confidence, and interpersonal relationships.

The family made a pact to raise money and worked together toward purchasing their own land, just like they had done back home. Each family member contributed to the collective effort, ensuring an equitable distribution of responsibilities. While working at such a young age, Nikki's legs began to give out, and she would notice veins popping out midday. Despite the pain, she pushed herself to keep going, knowing it was for her family's greater good. These struggles would follow her throughout her life, but she never gave up and continued to fight against adversity.

With the little time she had, Nikki dedicated it to her personal grooming. Her ability to hold a basic conversation in English and her unwavering work ethic helped her secure a job at a tomato harvesting plant. She quickly became well-liked by her colleagues and grew known for her diligence and intelligence. The owner of her workplace respected and admired her spirit, making Nikki his go-to person. He trusted her to relay messages to her family and the rest of the workers. Her hard work resonated within the family.

When in a foreign land, one wishes for their family members to work as a united front, providing unwavering support to one another. When a family stands together in the face of struggle and hardship, no force on earth can break them apart. Nikki understood the importance of relying on each other and finding joy in the small yet meaningful aspects of life. The family had moved to Yuba City with the determination and commitment to work hard and rise through the ranks until they could finally own their own property. Owning land in Yuba City was a significant achievement, signifying prestige and recognition, and Nikki intended to make it a reality for her family.

Nikki's infectious smile was unforgettable, but she was also admired for her strong personality. Being a woman of Eastern culture, her assertiveness wasn't always seen positively, but she persisted. She never let the opinions of others deter her from working relentlessly toward her goals. Nikki knew that tough times wouldn't last forever and maintained a positive outlook, giving her family hope and encouraging them never to give up easily. Such a self-aware person as Nikki doesn't just live a fulfilling and happy life themselves; their positivity is contagious and motivates those around them to reach for the stars.

"A woman with a voice is, by definition, a strong woman. But the search to find that voice can be remarkably difficult."

–Melinda Gates

Chapter 4: Embracing Challenges and Pursuing Dreams

Navigating through school life is no easy feat. The weight of assignments and the pressure to excel can often feel overwhelming, and some individuals even consider bypassing this phase altogether, jumping straight into the workforce. However, there are extraordinary individuals like Nikki who not only shoulder the responsibilities of a job but also embrace the additional challenge of education with unwavering determination.

Despite already having a challenging job that demanded her time, attention, and hard work, Nikki possessed a burning desire to further her education and pursue her dreams wholeheartedly. She exhibited remarkable resolve and purpose regarding academic and professional excellence.

As a foreigner now living in the United States full time, Nikki faced one of her biggest challenges in the form of language barriers. She could hold a very basic conversation but carrying out a full-on exchange was difficult. Adjusting to a new school was particularly tough due to this. There were moments when she found it challenging to understand what others were saying and had to ask them to repeat or speak more slowly. This was holding her back, and it was unlike Nikki to let this be. Determined, she devoted more time to refining her language and communication abilities to advance in her studies and career.

Despite her rigorous schedule, Nikki utilized her spare time for self-improvement. Whether working in the fields or studying, she prioritized personal grooming. She watched English movies and plays to enhance her fluency in the language and even purchased dictionaries and magazines to improve her linguistic skills further.

Throughout her time in school, Nikki faced the harsh reality of racism. She was subjected to bullying, labeled as a "dark-skinned Indian" girl, and faced derogatory comments about her appearance and nationality. This left her isolated and unable to forge friendships. However, Nikki never allowed the negativity to break her spirit. She wore a beautiful smile and radiated strength. While the hurtful comments occasionally troubled her, she refused to let them define her worth. Nikki carried her culture proudly to school, embracing her unique style and fashion choices. The criticism she faced only fueled her determination to grow stronger and rise above the prejudices she encountered. She remained an optimist, undeterred by negativity.

Nikki understood that achieving her dreams required hard work and perseverance. She faced additional challenges as an opinionated young woman in a traditional family. In a society where male dominance prevailed, she fearlessly made her own decisions and stood up for herself. Some people within her social circle were envious of her confidence and boldness, often taunting her for these qualities. But Nikki remained unswayed by their remarks, recognizing that their opinions held no place in her life.

Nikki's favorite subjects in school were Business Administration and Chemistry. She found joy in learning these subjects and devoted extra attention to them. Memorizing the periodic table became a playful game for her, singing it like a song throughout the day. The laboratory sessions were her favorite, where she witnessed chemicals reacting and observed unpredictable reactions with enthusiasm.

Nikki's English fluency improved as time passed. She confidently entered various places, engaging in conversations like any other individual. She recognized her English proficiency as the initial reward for her hard work and realized more rewards were on their way.

Despite her demanding job, Nikki prioritized studying, working countless nights toward achieving exceptional school grades. Her mother took extra care of her needs, understanding the sacrifices she was making for the family. On her days off, Nikki engaged in lengthy conversations with her parents, sharing her thoughts and dreams over a cup of tea. Such family moments became a cherished habit for her.

Nikki graduated high school with flying colors, instilling immense pride in her parents. As college life beckoned, she had to choose a professional path.

She then enrolled in a community college, pursuing her passion for business administration. Her commitment to excellence remained unwavering. Soon after college began, she embarked on a mission to obtain her driver's license, expanding her ability to support her family while still prioritizing her studies.

College life presented a new chapter for Nikki, one that was distinct from her experiences at school. Her exceptional academic skills and effective communication as an Indian quickly gained recognition. She excelled in her studies and eventually became a teaching assistant at the community college, sharing her knowledge and proficiency with others. Her hard work and dedication were appreciated by most teachers who recognized her contributions without racial bias. Business and leadership came naturally to her, and she understood that she was already a leader, building upon her family business. She saw her education as an opportunity to contribute further and drive the growth of the family enterprise.

Affording her education and supporting her family proved to be a real struggle. Nikki had to save every penny to pay her tuition and contribute to the family's living expenses. She had no room to indulge in luxuries like makeup and jewelry, prioritizing savings for her future goals instead. She gained a deeper understanding of the American dream, envisioning herself as a professional working alongside her American peers. Even during her most challenging moments, Nikki never lost sight of her determination to persevere, knowing she was the ray of hope for her family's brighter future. Her siblings also contributed their best efforts to support the family's aspirations, united in their strive for a better life.

Despite the meager savings, Nikki and her family understood the power of accumulation. Like raindrops contributing to fill the sea, their small savings had the potential to grow into a substantial sum in the future.

When Nikki was in college, her brothers' marriages were arranged in the traditional Indian manner. The family traveled to India, leaving Nikki behind to manage matters in their absence. During this time, Nikki had a car accident that left her shaken and terrified. Miraculously, she emerged from the incident unscathed. Perhaps the collective power of her parents' prayers and blessings shielded her from harm. The accident served as a profound reminder for Nikki that life is too short to be spent on pursuits devoid of passion. It strengthened her resolve to work even harder and achieve her dreams one by one. She embraced the incident as a source of motivation, propelling her further toward becoming the woman she aspired to be.

While living in a shared household with several families, Nikki contemplated securing a separate home for her immediate one. She recognized the challenges of saving enough money for such a venture but nonetheless shared her dream with her brothers. Nikki expressed her desire for them to save more diligently, acknowledging that they had all grown up. Her family appreciated her idea and resolved to work together to accumulate the necessary funds. After years of relentless hard work and struggle, Nikki and her siblings collectively saved $25,000, achieving the significant milestone of purchasing a new house. The moment was a dream come true for their family.

Chapter 5: A Journey of Marriage

The statement "being an opinionated girl in a brown family is definitely not for the light-hearted" struck a deep chord within me when I encountered it online. The phrase highlights the complexities that arise when Asian households, particularly Indian ones, support and protect their daughters while expecting them to conform to traditional roles. While Nikki did not have a hard time with this in particular, it was still a background reality, and she mustered through it with courage.

Although progress is being made today, not all Indian families embrace women's empowerment. What many fail to realize is that women are the mothers of humankind. Educating a single woman can save generations from illiteracy and lack of knowledge. Reflecting on my own experiences, I feel immense gratitude for being the son of a powerful woman who always believed in herself and stood tall during the darkest times of her life. My mother was kind and soft-spoken, yet she possessed a strong voice and made bold choices. I believe this quality contributed to her success in every aspect of her life. I am eternally grateful to the Supreme Power for blessing me with such a brave mother who recognized her worth from day one. She has always been unafraid to express her feelings and opinions.

Nikki's family held a special place in her heart, and she felt genuine gratitude and joy for having such incredible parents. They appreciated her hard work and unwavering hope, even in the face of adversity. Nikki's story taught me the importance of leaving behind valuable lessons and meaningful legacies for future generations. It reminds me that people are remembered for their words and actions that live on even after they leave this chaotic world.

In 1981, Nikki celebrated her twenty-third birthday, and according to her parents, it was the right age for her and her sister to consider marriage. Traditional Indian marriages were predominantly arranged then, with the couple's families playing a key role in the selection process. Interestingly, it was and still is majorly considered awkward and unethical for the prospective bride and groom to meet before their wedding night, especially in the presence of family members or relatives.

Belonging to a typical Indian family, Nikki accepted the concept of arranged marriage but disagreed with the tradition of not meeting the groom beforehand. She set a condition for her marriage that she would want the opportunity to meet the man her family had selected before making a final decision. Fortunately, her elders respected her wishes and agreed to arrange these meetings. In December 1981, Nikki and her family arrived in India after 7 years, and she experienced a whirlwind of emotions. She felt a mix of excitement, nervousness, tension, thrill, anxiety, and eagerness all at once. She was flooded with memories of her childhood friends and cousins. She embraced and cherished these memories, reminiscing about the joyful days she spent with her classmates at school. It was her first taste of true nostalgia, and she became emotional, overwhelmed by her feelings. Nikki remembered walking hand in hand with her father on the streets, visiting relatives' houses or local markets. Every detail of her early years came rushing back, and the nostalgia was palpable.

She reflected on how drastically her life had changed during those years. She took a trip down memory lane, recalling the successes, failures, accomplishments, and challenges that shaped her into a fearless individual. She felt a sense of pride in how far she had come since leaving India, never imagining that she would enjoy such stability and fulfillment in her life. She remained focused on her goals and learned from her past mistakes through all the ups and downs.

Nikki was determined to inspire others with her story and refused to settle for an ordinary life. She encouraged her friends and family to pursue their passions, believing that life was too short to be wasted on unfulfilling endeavors. She vowed to continue shining in every aspect of her life, spreading the magic of positivity, humility, and kindness wherever she went. She valued optimism and knew her own worth. She sought a partner who would bring happiness and respect into her life at all stages. Nikki couldn't believe she would return to the U.S. as a married woman. The most exciting chapter of her life was about to unfold, and amidst her fears and insecurities, she felt immense happiness embarking on this journey of marriage.

During their visit to India, Nikki and her sister explored their family's farm fields and orchards. They spent hours discussing their upcoming marriages, reminiscing about their childhood and the everyday chores they shared with their parents. Each moment rekindled countless memories. The fresh green grass and the scent of flowers evoked memories of the beautiful monsoon season when neighbors would come together to enjoy the rain. Nikki expressed her desire to marry a man who would respect her and her family and never treat them harshly.

About a week into the trip, Nikki's elders and brothers informed her that they had selected several men for her and her sister to consider for marriage. Nikki was shown several black-and-white pictures of the potential suitors. As she looked through the pictures, one young man caught her eye. Her face lit up, sensing a possible connection. There was a spark in his eyes that intrigued her. Nikki's brother explained that the young man, named Dave, belonged to a respectable family. Nikki was intrigued and sought a meeting before making any decisions. She believed it was wise to approach the idea of marriage with caution and ensure compatibility.

However, Nikki's plans did not unfold as anticipated. Interestingly, the initial meeting between Nikki and Dave did not occur privately. It took place in the presence of both families and close relatives. Dave and his family were invited to Nikki's house for the meeting and discussion if Nikki agreed to proceed. Although she couldn't properly speak with Dave due to the elders' presence, she made an effort to observe him discreetly. During the meeting, Nikki adorned traditional attire and covered her head with a scarf as a sign of respect for the elders.

While the elders engaged in conversation, Nikki and Dave sat silently, occasionally stealing glances at each other. Nikki, with her head bowed, observed Dave's sincere expression. She found comfort in the fact that Dave also sat respectfully and attentively listened to the elders. This gave her a positive impression and instilled mutual trust. Nikki could sense that Dave was a decent man who respected others and was of calm nature.

Although they couldn't have a private conversation, Nikki felt relieved simply having seen Dave in person. Prior to this meeting, she had only heard about him from her family. The single visit from Dave and his family left a positive impression on Nikki. She was impressed by his choice of words, soothing voice, and the respectful manner in which he interacted with his parents. All these observations led her to believe that Dave was a suitable match for her.

Similarly, Dave took the opportunity to observe Nikki in the presence of everyone. He wanted to ensure that the woman he intended to marry was ready for a marriage with someone from Punjab, India considering Nikki's formative years were in an advanced country like the USA. Dave wanted to ensure that the relationship was not imposed or forced upon her in any way. Something in Nikki's eyes convinced him that she was different from others. He sensed calmness and respect in her demeanor, and her body language showed no signs of disagreement or objection. This made Dave happy because he also liked Nikki. It was interesting how both parties noticed similar qualities in each other. Dave paid attention to how Nikki interacted with his parents, her choice of clothes, and the subtle amount of makeup she wore. All this analysis was done through an unspoken interaction.

Fortunately, during the conversation between the parents, Nikki's brothers remembered her wish to talk to Dave before the marriage. They urged her to have an initial discussion with him for her satisfaction. Although it was a brief conversation, it allowed Nikki and Dave to ask each other the questions they wanted. The meeting still took place in the presence of elders in the drawing room, but it allowed them to interact. After a short introduction and exchange of greetings, they mutually agreed to get married in January 1982, just a month away.

Both families were overjoyed with their decision. After Nikki whispered her "yes" in her mother's ear, she requested her father to finalize the commitment. In Indian tradition, families exchange sweets to congratulate each other after a couple makes a marriage commitment. The same happened in Nikki and Dave's case. As Dave and his family visited Nikki's house, her family served traditional Indian sweets called "mithai" and "laddoo" to everyone, symbolizing the acceptance of each other's proposals and as a token of shared happiness.

As soon as Dave's family left, detailed discussions about Nikki's wedding took place at home. The family planned a traditional "Desi wedding ceremony," where Nikki would wear a beautiful red outfit with elaborate makeup. They selected the perfect location for the event. The whole family eagerly went on shopping sprees to prepare for Nikki's wedding. Like any girl, Nikki wanted to dress up glamorously for her special day. Everyone accompanied her as they bought exquisite ornaments and expensive jewelry. It was customary in India to shower brides with household items, dresses, makeup, and jewelry during weddings.

Meanwhile, Dave's family also began their wedding preparations and celebrations. As typical Punjabis, they held traditional "dholki" sessions at their house, singing, dancing, and celebrating with family and friends. His parents dedicated their time to shopping for their daughter-in-law and son's special event. The wedding day approached in no time; four weeks had passed in a blink, and finally, the highly anticipated day arrived.

Interestingly, Nikki and her sister's weddings were scheduled just a day apart. Both sisters got married in the same month and year, with only a few hours between the ceremonies. The weddings were intimate affairs, with close family, friends, and relatives in attendance. Nikki and Dave exchanged vows in the presence of the holy Sikh scriptures, "Sri Guru Granth Sahib Ji," reciting religious mantras and receiving blessings for a happy married life. The ceremony followed a traditional Indian wedding format. Guests were treated to a delicious buffet in the garden, featuring a variety of flavorful dishes such as curries, salads, rice, bread, sweets, and drinks. Nikki's parents' home in the village was beautifully decorated with yellow lights, flowers, and glitter.

Nikki looked stunning in her traditional red attire, adorned with jewelry and makeup on the wedding day. Dave, dressed in his wedding attire and pagri, appeared as a typical Punjabi groom. Though not extravagant, the wedding was a joyous occasion, with everyone from Nikki's mother's house in the village attending and celebrating in true Sikh wedding style.

During their wedding night, Nikki, known for her strong will, initiated her first real conversation with Dave. The couple engaged in a detailed discussion about their happiness in choosing each other and what their future life would entail. Nikki was delighted to discover that Dave shared her ambition and discipline. He expressed genuine interest in her career and family plans. They talked all night about their shared life, including when they would move to the United States. Nikki had already decided to apply for Dave's nationality once they arrived in the U.S., as she wanted to support him in getting his parents and siblings to migrate permanently, too. Just like Dave, she wished for her in-laws to live with them, as she held them in high regard and respected Dave's mother for raising such a respectful son. Nikki felt overwhelmed by the love, gifts, and compliments she received from the entire family on her wedding day. She was the happiest woman in the world that day.

Chapter 6: A Journey of Sacrifice

Three months after their marriage, Nikki and Dave embarked on their new journey together, moving to the United States. With prayers and blessings from their elders and their hearts brimming with hope for the future, the couple was ready to commence their lives together.

Dave's unwavering support and devotion to Nikki made him an amazing husband and a true friend. He cherished Nikki for who she was and wholeheartedly embraced her choices. Witnessing her remarkable work ethic and ability to balance various roles in her life filled him with admiration. Nikki's love extended beyond their marriage, as she tenderly cared for her siblings and parents, exemplifying her nurturing nature.

The joyous news of Nikki's pregnancy arrived shortly after their arrival. This evoked a newfound excitement in them. Anticipation filled their hearts as they eagerly awaited the arrival of their child, a beacon of hope to greet them before the year's end. They did realize, however, that starting a family entailed additional responsibilities and financial demands. Like always, Nikki, driven by determination, set her sights high to provide a secure home for their growing family.

During the initial months, Nikki, recognizing the significance of their commitment to building a life together, encouraged Dave to obtain his driver's license. They toiled tirelessly on the farms saving every hard-earned penny for their future child. From April to December 1982, their relentless efforts yielded a remarkable $7,500—a testament to their resilience in the face of the prevailing minimum wage. With their savings goal successfully achieved, they discovered San Jose, a neighboring city teeming with burgeoning opportunities and entry-level jobs.

Alone, Dave embarked on a journey to San Jose, eager to seize the opportunities that awaited him. He appeared for multiple job interviews on a daily basis for a little while, but his hopes were shattered as he encountered rejections solely due to his turban-wearing Sikh appearance. This was the first time since their migration that Dave experienced racism, and it pierced his heart, for his hair held profound sacred significance in his religious beliefs. The thought of cutting his hair, a visible symbol of his identity and faith, weighed heavily upon him. Nikki's support shone through in this challenging moment, urging Dave not to compromise their religious and cultural values. The decision demanded immense sacrifice since it required him to summon the strength to let go of a cherished aspect of his heritage. Amidst the turmoil, Nikki's comforting words of assurance echoed in his ears, fueling his resolve to believe that brighter days lay ahead.

While Dave pressed on with his job search in San Jose, Nikki persevered on the farms, the weight of pregnancy on her body growing more tangible with each passing day. She remained steadfast, and her determination was fueled by the vision of a better life for their growing family.

December arrived, and with it came the much-anticipated birth of their daughter, my sister, Priti. Overwhelmed with joy, Dave hurried back from San Jose in the midst of interviews to be by Nikki's side, his heart brimming with indescribable happiness as he cradled his precious newborn daughter for the first time.

The couple rejoiced in Priti's birth, celebrating with reverence according to their cherished religious traditions. Surrounded by the love and unwavering support of their families, they were prepared to embark on the next chapter of their lives. Though a portion of their hard-earned savings went toward hospital fees and purchasing a car, they remained resolute in setting new goals to navigate the future that lay ahead.

With his spirit renewed with hope and determination, Dave returned to San Jose. This time, the tide of fortune turned in his favor as he secured a coveted job offer as a worker on the assembly line at

Apple Computers. Having left Nikki and Priti behind during this crucial time, Dave found the distance challenging, but they believed it was the right decision for their family's future. His job at Apple Computers marked a significant milestone—a stepping stone toward a brighter future, paving the way for their dreams to take flight.

After a month, Nikki recovered from her post-partum phase and joined Dave in San Jose, along with her sister and brother-in-law who they shared an apartment with to split expenses. Nikki and Dave were overjoyed to see each other after a month, but they had made a big sacrifice to make this reunion happen. They left their daughter Priti behind in Yuba City with Nikki's family so they could work and save enough money to start a new life. Understanding the challenges of managing her job in San Jose while also caring for her newborn, Nikki and Dave agreed that it would be best for Priti to stay with her grandparents for the first few months.

Nikki also started her career in Silicon Valley, venturing into an industry she knew little about. It was a challenging journey, but she had faced tougher times before. Dave and her family supported and encouraged her to build her career and afford a decent living in San Jose. Nikki managed everything independently, waking up early to prepare meals and handling household chores.

The couple would eagerly travel to Yuba City on weekends to see their daughter. Parting with her was a tough call to make, but it was a necessary sacrifice, driven by their aspiration to build a prosperous future for her in the new city. They worked long hours, including overtime, which was exhausting. Nikki was, at least, relieved knowing her daughter was in good hands with her mother providing a loving upbringing in her absence.

Following a year of residing with their extended family, Nikki and Dave moved into their very own apartment. This was more than a new dwelling; it was a space they could truly consider theirs. The move instilled in them a sense of achievement, even though a fully-fledged sense of security would only come with homeownership.

To ensure Priti could join them in their new residence, they meticulously planned their schedules. The prospect of their daughter reuniting with them after an entire year in a place that was theirs alone sparked a wave of excitement. They readied the apartment for Priti's arrival, arranging a makeshift crib and stocking up on toys. At long last, they were about to embark on living together, just the three of them, as a united family. The imminent reality of this filled Nikki with an overwhelming sense of joy. Now, they arranged their schedules to have one of them work while the other stayed at home with Priti. Nikki loved her new lifestyle, more so because she no longer had to wait for the weekends to be with her daughter. She had another reason to come home early every day. The couple cherished their new journey of parenthood, showering Priti with love and affection.

Nikki's life experiences serve as a lesson to women struggling to balance their personal and professional lives. Women go through numerous physical, emotional, mental, and social changes that are difficult to cope with. They often face pressure and have to sacrifice their own happiness for the sake of their children. It's never easy, but the key is to have faith in oneself, your beliefs, desires, and dreams. This confidence helped Nikki tremendously in her journey. She had unwavering faith in herself and the support of her loved ones.

Months passed by in a blink. As promised, Nikki helped her husband's family with immigration. Assisting Dave with the immigration process for his mother, Nikki ensured she would have help taking care of Priti. Once Dave's mother arrived, she assumed the caregiving role, freeing up Nikki and Dave to commit themselves to diligent work. Their single-minded aim: to amass enough savings to purchase their very own home. It was a true foundation for their family's growth, and having Dave's mother around was helpful. They worked long hours to meet their financial goals and, in just a couple of years, saved enough to make a down payment on a home in East San Jose, an area where their community was already established.

Shortly after settling into their new home, Nikki and Dave found comfort in the fact that several family members and friends also moved to the same area. The presence of familiar faces in the community brought a sense of security and belonging. As days passed, Nikki and Dave adjusted to their new neighborhood and had the opportunity to expand their network and make supportive friends. However, being a mother, Nikki remained vigilant about her child's safety. Considering her young age, she ensured Priti never played alone in the neighborhood.

The couple's struggle did not stop with having bought a house; they refocused their goals and worked toward them now. Dave dedicated himself to his work, striving to achieve further financial targets for the family. He wanted to provide Nikki and the children with all the comforts they deserved. He put in every effort possible to fulfill their needs. At the same time, Nikki continued to work toward her own dreams. She worked early hours and returned in the evenings, ensuring she equally contributed to the burden.

With enough savings, Nikki and Dave now applied for Dave's father and siblings to migrate. Fortunately, the process didn't take long, and their applications were approved relatively quickly. Soon after, the whole family reunited in the States to make their American dream a reality. It was an incredibly joyous moment for Dave, and he was grateful to be with his loved ones in such a beautiful country.

While it took some time for Dave's family to adjust to the new environment, everything eventually fell into place. In the meantime, Nikki and Dave provided support and shelter to their family members, helping them find suitable jobs and assisting them until they became financially stable. Dwelling together, they relished a period brimming with meaningful exchanges, weekend excursions on the open road, and the vibrant buzz of house gatherings.

During this time, Nikki thrived as a pure and happy soul. She made friends at work, and on her days off, she would explore new places around the neighborhood with them. Hosting events, gatherings, and parties became a regular occurrence at their new home. Nikki was outgoing and loved being part of the community. She never missed an opportunity to celebrate religious festivities and occasions. Each day brought new hope for a better future as she finally achieved financial stability after all the struggles and hardships. She had high aspirations for her future.

Around two years after moving into their new house, Nikki and Dave received the exciting news that they were expecting their second child. They were overjoyed and eagerly awaited the arrival of their new baby. Once again, this brought additional responsibilities. They knew they had to further manage their finances, save money, and effectively balance their time. They decided to continue working in shifts so one person could always be there for their children.

With her determined spirit, Nikki began planning and setting new goals for herself. She understood the importance of working harder and advancing in the Silicon Valley ladder. She became more focused on learning new technologies at work, enrolling in training sessions, seminars, and courses. The presence of her unborn child gave her a bright hope not only for her personal growth but also for her professional life. She had the confidence that everything would turn out well. Nikki shared the news of her pregnancy with her colleagues, who were also excited for her.

Throughout her second pregnancy, Nikki felt more at ease, knowing how to take care of herself during each trimester. She prioritized planning nutritious meals, including delicious Indian dishes like Sarson Da Saag, Makai Di Roti, and Lassi. With the support of her family, she managed household chores and ensured her comfort and happiness.

As Nikki neared the final stages of her pregnancy, she and Dave continued their diligent work schedule, accruing additional savings. Yet, recognizing the imminent arrival of their baby, they agreed it was time for Nikki to reduce her workload and focus on preparing for the newborn. She focused more on her spiritual practices and took daily walks. While she continued to work, she no longer took on overtime hours and prioritized her health and well-being.

The entire family was excited during this time. Nikki's mother checked in with her every day, ensuring she ate well and rested adequately. Her in-laws provided constant support and prepared delicious Punjabi meals. In the eighth month, Nikki and Dave made a shopping list for the baby, already having a good idea of what they needed. They went to the mall and happily shopped for their little one in the last few weeks until delivery, including fragrant baby oils, lotions, powders, and adorable clothes.

In May 1986, Nikki was nearing her due date, so she took maternity leave from work. The doctors advised her to stay home and go to the hospital immediately when she felt contractions or cramps. Dave remained beside Nikki, spending more time with her and their daughter, Priti. Nikki's mother-in-law tended to household work, including meals and cleaning, to sustain them for a couple of days. In June of 1986, as Nikki began to feel the onset of labor, the couple made a quick dash to the hospital. Dave reached out to both of their families, requesting their blessings and prayers for secure childbirth.

After a few hours, while Dave was praying in the waiting area with his mother, a nurse emerged from the ward, delivering the good news. Nikki had successfully delivered a baby boy, and that was none other than me! Overwhelmed with joy, Dave could barely find words to express his excitement. He thanked the nurse and eagerly inquired about Nikki's well-being. The nurse assured him she was doing well and he could see her soon.

They were delighted with my birth, and everyone celebrated this occasion. They named me 'Harman,' which means "everyone's beloved" in accordance with Punjabi tradition. With their precious daughter, Priti, and now, me, Nikki, and Dave felt complete. Their dream of welcoming two beautiful children into their lives had been fulfilled. Following tradition, Dave distributed sweets and laddoos to family and friends to celebrate their son's arrival.

Chapter 7: Taming the Unknown

Nikki knew she must excel professionally to achieve personal goals and push her family to further success. San Jose, California, was and is the heart of Silicon Valley. Without any technical knowledge or degrees, she knew she had to work hard to rise in a male-dominant industry. Nikki started her career in tech in 1983 as a supply chain worker in the semiconductor industry for a company called Integrated Device Technology, Inc. (IDT).

The semiconductor industry is the aggregate of companies engaged in designing and manufacturing semiconductors and related devices, such as integrated circuits. Nikki was initially employed as a supply chain worker at IDT, but it didn't take long for her managers to recognize her exceptional leadership skills. Within a short span of time, she was promoted to a supervisory position, overseeing a team of fifteen operators. This was a remarkable achievement only within the first year of her new career.

Under her new authority, Nikki prioritized operator workload, conducted employee evaluations, and provided training to production operators and new supervisors. She quickly discovered her passion for quality control and quality assurance, and she steadily grew within the field by gaining valuable experience and attaining relevant certifications.

Nikki's dedication to her work and her ability to connect with others extended beyond her professional responsibilities.

Nikki grew close to Debbie, a colleague at IDT, and they shared a great time working together. As per Debbie, Nikki's beautiful smile, bright eyes, and self-confidence immediately diffused any stress and created a comfortable working environment. She described Nikki as a natural team player, and the two quickly formed a tag team, divvying up the workload and ensuring efficiency. Beyond work-related discussions, they bonded over their shared love for Indian food. Knowing Debbie's vegetarian preference, Nikki often brought her delicious homemade lunches to work. Their lunch breaks became an opportunity to enjoy a meal together and talk about life, families, and their shared interests. Nikki even invited Debbie to her house, where she taught her how to cook some of her favorite Punjabi dishes. This gesture of friendship and warmth solidified their bond, and they became like sisters.

Debbie also shared her experiences attending Nikki's family functions with her husband. The Cherra family invited and welcomed them with open arms, making them feel like a part of the clan. The vibrant and exotic gatherings filled with colorful saris, dashing men wearing dastars (turban), and traditional dancing created a festive atmosphere. My paternal grandmother, who didn't speak English, also showed Debbie love and affection by stroking her hair and holding her hands. The love and inclusivity that permeated the Cherra home deeply touched Debbie, as she had not experienced such intimacy within her own family. Nikki's kindness and generosity knew no bounds, and she created a warm and loving environment wherever she went.

In the midst of their journey together, Nikki and Debbie stumbled upon a comical mishap that always left them in fits of laughter. It happened on an ordinary workday when Nikki, in a moment of distraction, accidentally poured a generous amount of Coke into the curry she had painstakingly prepared for their lunch. The initial surprise quickly gave way to uncontrollable giggles as they realized the unconventional blend of flavors they were about to experience.

Undeterred by the unexpected turn of events, Nikki and Debbie decided to embrace the situation with a sense of adventure. They sampled this curious mixture, allowing their taste buds to navigate the uncharted territory of carbonated curry. The fizzy tang of the Coke mingled with the spices, creating a peculiar yet oddly delightful fusion of flavors. With each bite, their laughter intensified, punctuated by sporadic burps that added an extra layer of amusement to their unforgettable lunchtime escapade.

The incident became a cherished memory, forever etched in their minds as a testament to their ability to find joy and laughter even in the most unexpected circumstances. It served as a reminder of the camaraderie and lightheartedness that defined their friendship, creating a bond that could weather any mishap, culinary-related or not, with grace and laughter.

Nikki's professionalism and integrity were highly regarded by her other colleagues at IDT too. Ron Thompson, one of her favorite QA managers, affectionately called her "Nicholas," a name she cherished. She had a natural ability to connect with others, fostering cohesion and integrity within any group or team she was a part of. Her colleagues respected her for her unwavering principles and ability to make tough choices, even if they were unpopular. Nikki fearlessly spoke the truth to the management, relying on her personal beliefs and principles to guide her. She gained the trust of her colleagues through her transparency and directness, never having a hidden agenda. Nikki's presence and contributions created an atmosphere of excellence and respect within the workplace.

After several years of personal and professional growth at IDT, Nikki felt capped in her role and embarked on a job search within the industry. Her determination led her to her next employer, Xilinx, Inc., where she would spend the next 15 years of her career. Xilinx became her second home—a place where she continued to climb the professional ladder, achieving her dreams and goals.

Cong, a coworker from Xilinx, shared his thoughts on Nikki's exceptional qualities. He described her deep devotion to her family, which she often shared stories about, showcasing her love and pride for her husband and children. Nikki's passion and intensity were remarkable, and she enthusiastically embraced each day. Interacting with people, diving headfirst into her work, and confronting challenging situations energized her. She possessed a rare ability to see people as individuals, valuing them for who they were rather than their titles or positions. Nikki treated everyone with compassion and respect, whether they were shipping clerks or the company's CEO. Her principled nature earned her the love and admiration of her colleagues.

Cong emphasized Nikki's integrity and her unwavering commitment to doing the right thing, regardless of the cost. At this company, too, she fearlessly spoke up, with her beliefs guiding her decisions, and time and again, she proved her assessments to be accurate. Nikki's self-reflective nature set her apart, as she constantly questioned herself and sought to ensure she was making the right choices. This level of introspection and genuine care was a rarity in the workplace, where many people merely clocked in and out for a paycheck.

Cong expressed his unwavering trust in Nikki, emphasizing the deep bond they shared. Despite her invaluable contributions to the workplace, Nikki remained humble and self-deprecating, never seeking attention or recognition for her achievements.

At Xilinx, Nikki's expertise in quality control and quality assurance flourished. She traveled extensively, performing audits across the globe. From Korea, Japan, and China to the Philippines, Australia, India, Canada, and various European destinations, Nikki gained a wealth of life experiences and professional growth. Her travels allowed her to immerse herself in different cultures and broaden her perspectives. These experiences shaped her into a well-rounded professional with a global mindset.

Chapter 8: Love Transcends Boundaries

Mothers hold a sacred place in our lives, serving as pillars of strength and guidance. Our mother, Nikki, embodied the epitome of beauty with brains, seamlessly blending her professional pursuits with her untiring dedication to her family.

In the earliest memories of our childhood, we recall the radiant smile that graced our mother's face, her flowing wavy hair, and her nurturing nature. She possessed an extraordinary ability to prioritize her family amidst the demands of a successful career, exemplifying the art of balance. As we grew up in the vibrant 1980s and 1990s, Nikki's love for us was expressed through her gentle but firm parenting style.

The family's narrative took a decisive turn with my birth, a landmark event that coincided with our relocation to a new home—destined to be our haven for many years. This period of transition marked a profound shift in our family dynamics as we left the comfort of the shared space with cherished family members and initiated a new phase of life that demanded the exploration of uncharted territories. Priti and I, aged 9 and 6 respectively at the time, found ourselves adapting to a multitude of firsts—embracing a new neighborhood, enrolling in a new school, and forging new friendships. While it was a time of adjustment, our parents provided us with constant support and prepared us for the challenges that lay ahead.

Nikki's continued dedication to her family was evident from the break of dawn. Each morning, she would get up before everyone else, carefully braiding Priti's hair at 5:30 am and then making us lunch. After that, she ensured Dave would drop us off at school while she headed to work. She consciously scheduled her work timings to ensure she was home when we returned from school. This routine persisted for years, fortifying our familial bond and forging an unbreakable unity.

On Saturdays, our family eagerly participated in the deep cleaning ritual set forth by my mother. Each member contributed their share to restore our home's immaculate order. I took charge of disposing of trash and tidying my toys, gradually assuming greater responsibilities as I grew older. Priti lent a hand in cleaning the bathroom and folding laundry, learning the art of domestic duties. Nikki meticulously dusted and swept while Dave tackled the vacuuming and mopping.

As the years passed, Nikki's career soared to new heights, necessitating domestic and international travel ranging from a couple of business days to extended two-week trips. Recognizing the importance of independence and self-sufficiency, my mother also found it vital to teach us essential life skills, including cooking and laundry. In an effort to further our culinary learning, my father took the initiative to build a kitchen in our garage. This act was yet another affirmation of their unwavering commitment to our empowerment.

Despite her demanding career, Nikki yearned to be the quintessential "soccer mom." She wholeheartedly supported and attended our sporting events and educational endeavors, encouraging us to diligently pursue our dreams. Her message to us was clear: No dream was too small, and success could be achieved through wholehearted commitment. Though Nikki herself hadn't had the opportunity to attend a four-year college, she imparted her wisdom, emphasizing the importance of education and personal growth. Her words resonated deeply within us, shaping our perspective on life.

Our home, under my mother's warm embrace, was a sanctuary for love and hospitality. She enjoyed hosting family members, whether it was her siblings, nieces, nephews, or friends. Nikki's culinary prowess was renowned, and she delighted in experimenting with new recipes and flavors; her love for cooking was evident in every dish she served.

Amidst her own busy life, my mother never lost sight of her parents' well-being. Each day, during her commute from work, she diligently made phone calls to her parents and siblings, bridging the physical distance with love and care. She cherished the connection with her family and became their pillar of support. Whenever distress befell her parents or siblings, Nikki's compassionate nature propelled her to step in and assist. One remarkable act of her kindness was purchasing a house in San Jose, ensuring her parents and younger brother could lead a more comfortable and secure life.

Having traversed the world on her own and going on adventures, my mother yearned to share her experiences with her children, creating unforgettable memories on foreign soil. Family trips to England, France, and India became commonplace and cherished chapters in our lives, opening our eyes to the wonders of different cultures and fostering a sense of appreciation for the world's diversity.

As the years passed, the bond between Nikki and Priti deepened, giving rise to countless mother-daughter moments. They reveled in the joy of giving each other manicures and pedicures, relishing in the simple act of pampering and nurturing. These moments of shared bliss brought immeasurable happiness and contentment, filling our hearts with love and strengthening our connection. Shopping escapades were always memorable, with fitting room fashion shows transforming mundane tasks into delightful adventures.

The sands of time continued to flow, and the moment for Priti to embark on her college journey arrived—a significant milestone for both, her and our family. Though filled with mixed emotions, our parents instilled in Priti the confidence to embrace her independence, empowering her to become a strong, capable young woman. Nikki's unwavering support and belief in Priti's abilities catalyzed her success.

A few years later, it was my turn to leave the warmth of our family home and venture into a four-year college experience along the enchanting California Coast. Our parents, once again, grappled with a whirlwind of emotions as they bid farewell to their youngest child. Yet, they understood this was a necessary step toward personal growth and independence. Their constant belief in our potential and their unyielding love provided the foundation for our journeys.

Upon our respective graduations, Priti and I returned home, reuniting as adults. Our relationship dynamics with Nikki transformed as she transitioned from being a mother to our best friend. We shared laughter, tears, and cherished memories as her enduring love and constant support continued to shape our lives.

Chapter 9: A Journey of Dedication and Impact

After years of dedicated service, it was time for Nikki to make a difficult decision— leave Xilinx, the company where she had thrived for a significant portion of her career. Tendonitis at her elbow had taken its toll on her, making it increasingly challenging to continue in her role. It was a turning point in her life as she was finally going to retire and focus on her well-being.

Retirement, however, wasn't the fulfilling experience Nikki had envisioned. The absence of work left her feeling unfulfilled and yearning for a sense of purpose. It was during this period of reflection that she realized her passion for her profession was still very much alive. With a renewed spirit, Nikki embarked on a new chapter, seeking contract assignments to keep her engaged and active in her field.

Unfortunately, Nikki soon discovered that the world of contractual work didn't align with her values and work style. The lack of stability and the constant need to prove herself in new environments didn't sit well with her. She longed for a deeper connection and the opportunity to make a lasting impact. And so, she set her sights on Abbott Labs, a renowned organization where she believed her wealth of knowledge and expertise could truly shine.

At Abbott, my mother's professional reputation preceded her. Her former manager, Kevin, provided a glowing testimonial about her exceptional work ethic, professionalism, and genuine care for her colleagues. From the moment she joined Abbott in 2008, it was evident that Nikki approached the position with full dedication and a commitment to excellence.

Nikki's contributions were nothing short of remarkable within the Supplier Quality team at Abbott. She seamlessly collaborated with various functional groups, including Supplier Quality, Manufacturing/Operations, Technical, Purchasing, and Supply Chain. Her ability to build synergy among these groups led to enhanced efficiency and improved processes.

One aspect that Nikki significantly impacted was addressing the water testing issues in collaboration with the technical team. Her expertise and attention to detail were instrumental in resolving these challenges, ensuring that quality standards were consistently met. Her commitment to delivering excellence extended beyond her immediate responsibilities.

She played a pivotal role in streamlining the supplier base, working closely with the purchasing group to assess and reduce redundancies in the materials and products utilized. This optimization resulted in cost savings and improved overall supplier management—a testament to Nikki's strategic thinking and ability to drive impactful change.

Furthermore, Nikki's dedication to excellence transcended the boundaries of her job description. She willingly ventured into uncharted territories to assist colleagues and ensure the success of the department and business goals. Her vast knowledge and experience allowed her to provide valuable input to QA and operations engineering, overcoming obstacles and finding innovative solutions.

One of Nikki's notable achievements was spearheading the Electrostatic Discharge (ESD) improvement project within the Material Review Board. By implementing preventive measures, she successfully minimized ESD failures of printed circuit boards, contributing to improved product quality and reliability.

Nikki's contributions weren't limited to internal operations alone. She conducted meticulous on-site supplier evaluations, documenting her findings and establishing strong relationships with suppliers. Through effective communication and prompt resolution of quality issues, she fostered a collaborative and efficient supplier network that benefited the entire organization.

Moreover, Nikki's dedication to her profession went beyond her individual accomplishments. Recognizing the value of mentorship and leadership, she actively guided and supported her peers within the Supplier Quality team. Her mentorship had a lasting impact, elevating the performance of the entire group and fostering a culture of continuous improvement and shared success.

Through Nikki's tireless efforts, Abbott's Santa Clara site underwent several external audits without any observations within the Supplier Quality Management. Her meticulous attention to documentation accuracy and commitment to excellence played a vital role in maintaining the highest standards.

As she reflected on her career journey, Nikki realized that her professional achievements were not solely about personal success but also about making a positive difference in the lives of others. The fulfillment she derived from helping her colleagues grow and creating a supportive work environment was immeasurable. It was this realization that fueled Nikki's continued passion for her work as she eagerly looked forward to the next chapter of her career, armed with the knowledge that her contributions had left a lasting impact on the organizations she served.

With an unwavering dedication to excellence, a wealth of experience, and a heart filled with compassion, Nikki's journey continued to evolve. She embraced new challenges, sought growth opportunities, and remained committed to making a positive difference wherever she went. The impact she had on her colleagues, the organizations she served, and the field she loved was a testament to her undying spirit and her constant dedication to excellence. And as she embarked on each new chapter, my mother carried with her the lessons learned, the relationships built, and the lasting legacy of a true leader and changemaker.

Chapter 10: A Sanctuary of Dreams

As my sister Priti and I journeyed into early adulthood, we began to witness profound changes in our mother, Nikki. This transformation was most evident in her shifting perspective on pets. During the days of our youth, Nikki stood as the embodiment of structure and discipline, the resolute sentinel who maintained order and ensured that household rules were steadfastly adhered to. Yet, as the sands of time slipped through our fingers, we began to witness the emergence of a more tender side of her. Layers of her personality, previously masked by her authoritative demeanor, now began to unfold, giving us more profound insights into the multifaceted woman who raised us.

Growing up, Priti and I harbored a childhood dream: a pet dog to call our own. Despite our heartfelt requests and vows of responsibility, Nikki would gently steer us toward understanding the significant commitment a pet demanded. To an outsider, it might have appeared that she held a personal aversion to animals. However, that couldn't have been further from the truth.

During late-night conversations, Nikki would often reminisce about her childhood in Yuba City, sharing tales of the animals she encountered. Through these stories, we learned of her family's cherished pets and her understanding of the inherent responsibilities. It became clear that her resistance wasn't due to a lack of affection but from a place of protection. She wanted to shield us from the heartbreak of potentially not being able to care adequately for a pet.

The familial dynamics saw a dramatic shift during my final year of undergraduate studies when a pet-related incident turned our household rules on their head. I had accompanied a friend to a local dog shelter, a place buzzing with canines in various stages of their lives. Amidst the orchestrated chaos of dogs energetically feeding or playing, one small, neglected puppy in a corner tugged at my heartstrings.

Despite food being laid out before him, the puppy sat still, trembling, and distant from the lively atmosphere around him. On further inquiry, I learned about the puppy's history of abuse. It was a revelation that echoed within me, sparking a connection I hadn't anticipated. Acting on impulse, I decided to bring this little one home.

I named him Bentley.

The prospect of introducing Bentley into our traditionally no-dog household was daunting. I was poised on the verge of graduation, and returning home to live with my parents was a looming reality. But, I took a leap of faith and relayed Bentley's story to Nikki over a phone call, sharing my decision to adopt him.

To my utter surprise, Nikki's reaction wasn't one of stern disapproval as I had anticipated. Instead, her words were laced with understanding and empathy. Not only did she welcome Bentley into our home, but she also reassured me that our home would always be Bentley's as well. This unexpected revelation of Nikki's empathetic nature was heartwarming to experience.

From the moment Bentley and Nikki first met, there was an unmistakable aura of enchantment in the air. The introduction, filled with anticipation, blossomed into an instant, heartwarming connection. Nikki took Bentley into her arms and heart, embracing him as though he had always been an integral member of our family. It was as if she'd been waiting for him all along, and now that he was here, a void was filled.

The depth of Nikki's affection for Bentley wasn't limited to the confines of our home. Each day, she found joy in recounting the little antics and tales of Bentley to anyone who'd listen - be it her colleagues at work, friends she met, or even casual acquaintances. Nikki's face would light up with pride and joy every time she shared his stories, whether it was his first bark, a playful chase around the garden, or a new trick he had learned. It became evident that

Bentley wasn't just a pet; he was now an inevitable part of the family.

With Bentley's arrival, one of the more remarkable transformations in Nikki pertained to her erstwhile reservations about pets indoors. Nikki, with her penchant for cleanliness, was always wary of the inevitable shedding that came with dogs. In her earlier perspective, the idea of tufts of hair adorning the furniture or carpet was less than ideal. However, Bentley, primarily an indoor dog, seemed to dissipate all those apprehensions. The day he trotted into our home, Nikki's reservations about pet hair vanished. The occasional strand of Bentley's hair found on the couch or her clothes became not a matter of nuisance but a gentle reminder of the furry bundle of joy that had come into their lives.

And then, there were those heartwarming moments where Nikki and my dad, Dave, would take on the role of doting grandparents. Together, they'd lovingly bathe and groom Bentley, taking turns ensuring he looked his best. Their meticulous care, the gentle lathering of soap, the soft brushing of his fur, and the pride in their eyes after each session were a testament to the deep bond they shared with Bentley. It wasn't just a routine but a labor of love akin to doting grandparents fussing over a cherished grandchild. The sight of them, engrossed in their care for Bentley, became one of the family's treasured visuals, symbolizing unconditional love and affection.

As I delved deeper into my professional doctoral studies in San Jose, the dynamics between my parents, Bentley, and myself began to undergo a beautiful transformation. San Jose, with its familiar streets and warmth, became a haven where our familial ties flourished. My days took on a rhythmic cadence, interlaced with Nikki's pearls of wisdom during our lengthy conversations, the tantalizing aroma of Indian dishes she whipped up, and Bentley's effervescent presence always lighting up the room.

Under Nikki's watchful eyes, I was not only mastering the delicate art of Indian culinary traditions but also juggling the manifold responsibilities that came with being part of an extended family. Though such a living arrangement had its fair share of intricacies and demands, our shared values and deep-seated respect for one another transmuted potential hurdles into moments of growth and understanding. Our bonds deepened, weaving an intricate tapestry of love, trust, and mutual support.

Our home in San Jose became the backdrop for countless memories, each moment painting its unique stroke on the expansive canvas of our shared journey. The year 2010 ushered in a significant decision— renovating our home to accommodate our growing family better. Amidst the frenzy of construction blueprints, material selections, and countless meetings with contractors, Bentley remained our unwavering beacon of joy, his antics and affection often serving as the perfect antidote to a day's fatigue.

Yet, as 2011 dawned and we enthusiastically plunged into the intricacies of our home transformation, a subtle shift in the atmosphere began to creep in. The narrative of Nikki's life, which we had always associated with tenacity, resilience, and moments of joy, seemed on the cusp of an unforeseen twist. A looming revelation threatened to unsettle the equilibrium of our familial harmony. With bated breath, we faced the possibility of an event so profound that it might redefine the contours of our collective existence, casting its elongated shadows over the promises of tomorrow and ushering us into an uncharted realm of challenges and change.

Chapter 11: Resilience Amidst Storms

March 2011 presented an evening that transformed our ordinary lives into a challenging saga. Our family's otherwise active and healthy matriarch, Nikki, had been complaining of continuous stomach discomfort and bloating. After an immediate yet thorough abdominal examination at home, I identified the telltale signs of ascites, a fluid accumulation in the abdomen. My heart raced with trepidation; her symptoms pointed to an ominously serious health issue. Our next step was clear - we needed immediate professional attention, which led us to the Kaiser Emergency Room. This role reversal starkly contrasted our routine hospital visits, where my mother would accompany me for my checkups.

After conducting various blood tests and imaging studies, we waited in uncomfortable silence, the calm before the storm. Our conversations, a meager attempt at normalcy, revolved around home renovations and mundane daily affairs, as we anticipated the results with bated breath. Soon, the doctor entered the room, computer in hand, laden with reports and the gravity of the news he was about to deliver.

The persistent echo of my mother's teachings, *"Always hope for the best, and prepare for the worst,"* which had filled our house for as long as I could remember, now reverberated in the tense silence of the examination room. The comforting wisdom of her words took on a haunting reality when the doctor, with an air of professional detachment, pronounced the life-altering diagnosis:

"There's a malignancy."

While my heart skipped a few beats at the words, my mother's response was awe-inspiring. Her exterior, calm and composed, served as a brave façade for the emotional storm within her. Her unwavering strength bolstered us as we navigated the deserted San Jose streets at 2 am. She articulated her plan to combat the diagnosis with resilience and a pinch of humor, terming the cancer *"cookies."*

"We will call it 'cookies,' Harman, and we are going to make every single cookie crumble," she declared with resolute determination. In her eyes, what might have been viewed as an unbeatable adversary was a challenge to face head-on. Her perspective, so uniquely hers, humanized the grave medical diagnosis, transforming it from a shadowy fear into a tangible obstacle we were determined to overcome.

Resting in my bed, the haunting stillness of the night enveloped me. Each time I closed my eyes, I was thrust back into the cold, sterile room, the piercing lights, and the somber expressions of the medical staff. Phrases that once seemed relegated to textbooks and distant patients, like "malignancy" and "metastasis," now loomed large in my consciousness. They echoed in my mind, threatening to drown out every other thought. The sheer magnitude of the diagnosis, further solidified by the CT scan's findings, pressed down on me with a weight that seemed almost too immense to bear. Every whispered rumor and every hushed conversation I'd ever heard about the devastating effects of cancer surged to the forefront of my mind.

In the midst of this storm of anxiety and fear, a beacon of hope shone through: the unwavering spirit of my mother, Nikki. Seeking comfort and perhaps a semblance of understanding, I slowly made my way to her room. The soft glow from her bedside lamp revealed her contemplative face. As I approached, our eyes met, and without a word, I reached out, our fingers intertwining. That simple gesture, the warmth of her hand enveloping mine, communicated more than words ever could. It was a testament to our unbreakable bond, a promise that no matter how treacherous the journey ahead, we would face it hand in hand.

The next chapter of our lives promised to test our resolve, our endurance, and the very fabric of our familial bond. The road that lay ahead was strewn with uncertainties and potential heartbreaks. Yet, in the face of this adversity, a resolute belief emerged:

Together, bolstered by a lifetime of shared memories and an undying love, we would navigate this challenging terrain. Our family's unwavering spirit and boundless resilience would be our guiding light, leading us through even the darkest of times.

Chapter 12: The Dawn of an Unforeseen Battle

The following morning dawned bright, though the day promised to carry a weight we were unprepared for. With the stark realities of last night still raw and overwhelming, we dressed in the armor of resilience and prepared to face the day.

As we all sat around the breakfast table, my mother turned to my father, who was just about to leave for work. In her calm yet firm voice, she held him back. There was a gravity in her words that brooked no argument; we needed to discuss the events of the last night, the dark revelations that had unfolded within the sterile confines of the hospital.

It was a surreal moment, speaking the dreaded diagnosis aloud. It left an unusual silence in the room. We told Dave about the malignant cells spreading insidiously within Nikki's body. The cancer, we explained, was assumed to be originating from her ovaries based on the ascites and preliminary imaging studies. The news was like a punch to the gut to Dave, a brutal blow that shattered the protective bubble of our happy, peaceful life.

As the news sunk in, the sounds of the ongoing house renovation seemed almost a mockery, a stark contrast to the upheaval within our hearts. The initial impulse was to halt the project to divert all our focus toward Nikki's health. Yet, in her true fashion, she remained steadfast. She insisted we continue with our lives normally, her strength and determination refusing to let cancer dictate our course.

Standing shoulder to shoulder with her, I solemnly pledged to be her partner in this battle, her rock in these troubled times. We let our extended family in on our secret, preparing them for the emotional rollercoaster we were about to embark on. However, there was a caveat - there were to be no signs of sorrow or despair in Nikki's presence. We needed to project strength, positivity, and resilience to nurture the same spirit in Nikki. We wanted to keep her luminous smile undimmed, her spirit unbroken.

While we were navigating these tumultuous waves, Nikki made a simple request. She humbly asked us to maintain our usual demeanor around her, to keep our faces fresh and our spirits high.

The difficult task of sharing the news with my sister, Priti, who was living in San Diego, fell upon me. Breaking the news to her and listening to her heart shatter over the phone was one of the hardest conversations I've ever had. Yet, she held on, promising to catch the next flight back to be with us.

In the following days, Nikki and I embarked on a series of medical consultations, fully comprehending the gravity of her condition and the path that lay before us. The team of medical specialists meticulously outlined the intricacies of her case, shedding light on the significance of the primary tumor nestled within her ovaries. They emphasized the necessity of an aggressive surgical intervention known as debulking or cytoreductive surgery, a pivotal first step in managing advanced ovarian cancer.

The primary objective of debulking surgery is to excise as much of the tumor as possible, striving to eradicate any visible signs of cancer. Extensive research has demonstrated that this approach significantly enhances survival rates and improves overall outcomes for patients grappling with advanced ovarian cancer. The surgeon, a distinguished gynecologic oncologist, expounded upon the surgical plan with meticulous detail, refraining from staging the cancer until the results of the surgery and subsequent biopsies were available. As we prepared to leave the hospital, Nikki was thoughtfully provided with pain medications to ensure her comfort and a date for the surgery was promptly scheduled for the following week.

Reflecting on the unfolding events, I remembered Nikki's proactive approach to her health. She was always vigilant about changes in her body, ensuring regular check-ups for even minor symptoms. In the years leading up to her diagnosis, she had experienced occasional post-menopausal bleeding, which she diligently got examined.

However, ovarian cancer is often referred to as the 'silent killer.' Its symptoms are non-specific and often mimic common ailments. Many women, including healthcare providers, can mistake these symptoms for menopause, dietary issues, stress, or functional bowel problems. This insidious nature of the disease often leads to late diagnoses.

As we came to terms with our new reality by the end of the week, we acknowledged there was no time for sorrow. We were at war with an invisible enemy, and our best weapons were love, resilience, hope, knowledge, and action. We laid out our plan to the family, preparing them for the challenges ahead. I decided to take a sabbatical from my graduate studies, dedicating full attention to supporting Nikki through this ordeal.

Finally, the day of the surgery arrived. Dressed in her hospital gown, Nikki lay in the pre-operative room, her face wearing a brave mask of stoic resolve. As the anesthesiologist and the obstetrician-gynecologist (her surgeon) entered the room, I stood by her side, my arms crossed, attentively listening to their discussion. Mid-sentence, they stopped and acknowledged my presence. At that moment, a warm sense of reassurance flooded Nikki. She was not alone in this battle; she had a steadfast companion right there, next to her. A companion who was ready to face the storm head-on.

As informed, the surgery was going to be a long, complex process that could last anywhere between eight to ten hours.

For the entire duration, once it started, our family held a quiet vigil in the waiting room. Dad, Priti, and I, along with some other close family members, were rooted to our seats, anxiously pacing, watching the screens for any update about Nikki.

Five hours into the surgery, the surgeon stepped out of the operating room. Seeing him so early sent a chill of dread down our spines. But he immediately put us at ease, explaining that the surgery was progressing well and most of the debulking procedure was complete.

He took his time describing the surgery's complexity and how widespread the tumors were. A surgical cut spanning the length of Nikki's abdomen was made out of necessity. His words stressed the importance of caring for her wound during recovery. I listened, absorbing every word, keen on understanding the exact nature of my mom's condition.

When we finally got to see her post-surgery, the relief was indescribable. The first, most challenging hurdle of her battle had been overcome.

For the following nights, I kept a watch by her side. The postoperative pain was intense, causing her to whimper through the night. I stayed awake with her, holding her hand and providing comfort in those grueling hours.

The nursing staff was generally efficient and kind, but occasionally, they were inadvertently rough, causing Nikki unnecessary discomfort. I practically made it my job to ensure they were informed about her sensitivities, especially during shift changes.

After several nerve-wracking days at the hospital, we finally brought our mother to the comfort of a home. We transformed the place into a sanctuary of care for her, catering to every need she might have.

Despite the challenging circumstances, we drew strength from each other, ready to face what lay ahead. Our resilience grew as the days turned into nights and then back into days, paving the way for the battle that awaited us.

Chapter 13: Finding Light in the Darkness

The day that loomed heavily over our heads was finally upon us. The pathology results were ready, and it was time to face what we had spent countless hours fretting about. With steely resolve, Mom and I ventured to the oncologist's office. We walked in together, side by side, mirroring each other's determined stride and hopeful glances. Mom was Nikki that day, not a patient but a woman - strong, brave, and ready to face her truth.

The room was sterile, medical diplomas decorating the walls, bearing silent witness to the pivotal conversations that took place within its confines. The oncologist's voice echoed, bouncing off the white-washed walls, filling the room with the solemn truth: Stage 3C ovarian cancer, with a five-year prognosis. A profound silence followed the revelation. Time was suspended at the moment as we absorbed the weight of his words.

We were standing on the edge of a precipice, staring down at a chasm filled with uncertainty and challenges. Nikki, however, exhibited extraordinary resilience, like always. She decided that we should bear the brunt of the news ourselves. We would shoulder the severity, shielding our family from the harshness of the diagnosis to keep their spirits encouraged and their hope alive.

The standard treatment, chemotherapy, began shortly after. Six cycles, each administered every 21 days, using a cocktail of drugs designed to battle the ugly disease. We braced ourselves for what was to come as a result of this therapy, nausea, exhaustion, hair loss, and skin and nail problems. Nikki bore it all with endurance, her determination unwavering.

Nighttime brought its own challenges. Mom's legs were wracked with discomfort. In the stillness of the night, our home was filled with the low hum of whispered prayers and the rhythmic kneading of hands massaging her aching legs. Our family banded together, sharing the responsibility of providing comfort and care to her.

Chemotherapy began to show its signs. Nikki's body, once robust and lively, began to thin. And then there was the hair, her precious locks, that began to fall out in patches. She was someone who had always carried her hair like a crown and elegantly styled and tended to them with great care. She took control of the narrative due to changing circumstances and instructed me to shave her head, a defiance of the disease trying to strip her of her identity.

With Nikki's newly-shaved head, we found a different kind of beauty and strength emanating from her. She glowed with defiance and resilience, her bare head a testament to her unwavering spirit. But, she was not done.

Next came the wig shopping, a journey of reinvention and an act of reclaiming control. We spent hours navigating the labyrinth of wigs, each offering a new persona and opportunity for expression.

This chapter of our lives was marked by raw honesty, the strength of familial bonds, and resilience in the face of adversity. It was a testament to Nikki's incredible spirit and her determination to shape our narrative, focusing on hope and unity rather than despair and fragmentation. Through it all, she remained an embodiment of courage, inspiring us all with her indomitable spirit.

Meanwhile, our house remained a symphony of hammer strikes and sawdust. One might imagine that the construction, a display of disorder, could burden Nikki. Yet, quite contrary to our expectations, it was a hidden blessing. The renewal that was happening to our house was akin to the internal revolution Nikki was experiencing. The transformation of our home became a beacon of positivity for Nikki, a tangible demonstration of change and rebirth, a testament to the notion that chaos often sprouts a new beginning.

On the days when Nikki felt stronger, unfettered by the punishing aftermath of chemotherapy, we would travel to local stores to shop for construction materials. From marble tiles to countertops, carpeting to lighting, Nikki relished in the process of creation. The joy that filled her eyes as she browsed through the aisles, choosing items to construct the home she always desired, was heartwarming. It was a break from the world of medication and pain, a glimpse into a more mundane yet cherished life she once knew.

Nikki wasn't merely a spectator in this transformation; she was its architect. Her active participation in the construction and with the workers further underscored her strength and indomitable spirit. She fostered relationships with them, offering water and snacks daily, turning the professional relationship into a friendly rapport. Through these acts of kindness, it was as if she was pouring a piece of herself into the home's foundation, embedding her spirit within the walls.

It was a testament to the woman Nikki always was: kind, strong, and resilient. The house, much like its lady, was undergoing a transformation, shaping up to be a sanctuary of hope and rejuvenation.

Chapter 14: Dancing with Shadows and Sunshine

With Nikki's courage as her anchor, she weathered the relentless waves of chemotherapy. A respite came when the ominous clouds of cancer showed signs of scattering. Her medical reports bore optimistic news: her CA125 levels had significantly dwindled, and PET scans showed diminishing signs of the sinister malignancy. This was a victory, a hard-earned relief in the face of a formidable adversary.

Nikki gradually began to reclaim her vitality. Like a fragile sapling pushing through a crack in a concrete jungle, her recovery was slow yet resolute. Her iron-willed spirit compelled her to return to her professional life at Abbott soon after. She didn't perceive her work as just a means of livelihood but rather as a comforting space of kinship and joy amidst her personal whirlwind.

Her colleagues greeted her return with warmth and camaraderie. Their bond offered her a sanctuary and a semblance of normality amidst the tumultuous upheaval in her life. Their companionship filled her days with laughter, positivity, and a sense of belonging.

Simultaneously, our home, a mere blueprint of dreams in the not-so-distant past, had beautifully blossomed into reality. The finished product was a testament to our collective perseverance and resilience, much like Nikki's own journey. Every brick laid and every wall erected mirrored our shared fortitude and optimism.

Our home reverberated with love, laughter, and spirited exchanges. There were impromptu dance-offs, with my mother swaying to the beats of her beloved Punjabi music, her infectious laughter lending music to our lives. We celebrated life and shared precious moments, recognizing the uncertainty of what lay ahead.

While we reveled in the respite, we remained mindful of Nikki's health. Routine blood tests and PET scans were an integral part of our lives, knowing all too well that the prognosis hinged on the specter of recurrence.

Six months into remission, the unwanted guest returned. The creeping CA125 levels signaled the recurrence of cancer, plunging us back into the fray. Nikki, as always, remained undeterred. She resumed her chemotherapy sessions, ready to combat the recurrent adversary with unyielding determination.

She resumed work that was temporarily paused during treatment as soon as she gained strength. Cancer was not a controller of her life; it was merely a chapter. My mother's spirit was indomitable, radiating a glow of hope and resilience for us all to draw upon.

Despite the arduous struggle, Nikki's infectious smile never wavered. Her lessons, shared through countless conversations and the silent language of her courage, imparted wisdom that no classroom or textbook could offer. Her battle wasn't just against cancer; it was a lesson in the art of living and loving, even in the face of danger.

As I reached the pinnacle of my academic journey, finally earning my doctorate, my mother's joy knew no bounds. Our home echoed with the melody of her jubilant dances and the resonance of shared laughter.

Cancer, for Nikki, was an unwelcome guest that kept revisiting. The disease retreated, only to return, trapping us in a cyclical dance of anguish and hope. Through this, Nikki became a seasoned warrior, combatting cancer with a spectrum of treatment drugs, each with its unique set of challenges and promises. But, each recurrence met with Nikki's unyielding spirit, her resilience undeterred, her courage unwavering.

She wasn't alone in her journey. Together with me, we became active members of her healthcare team. Our rapport with the medical doctors at Kaiser transcended traditional roles, fostering an alliance built on mutual respect and shared objectives.

This bond extended beyond clinical discussions. It also encompassed frequent phone consultations where we collectively strategized her treatment, a joint mission to sail through the stormy sea of her disease.

While medical treatments formed the cornerstone of Nikki's fight, she also sought complementary methods to fortify her body. A lifestyle transformation ensued, encompassing dietary changes, regular exercises, hyperbaric oxygen therapy, and immune-boosting protocols, all guided and supported by her medical team.

Nikki, despite her condition, lived her life to the fullest. She attended weddings, functions, and gatherings, her spirit undiminished by her disease. Her presence remained the glue that held our family together, spreading love and warmth amidst our collective struggle.

Through it all, Nikki's resilience was more than an act of survival; it was an inspiration that transformed our lives. Through her journey, we learned that regardless of the darkest nights, the promise of a new dawn was never far away.

Chapter 15: Treasuring Moments

Despite the tumultuous waves that threatened to capsize her, Nikki remained a beacon of resilience, her spirit refusing to dim. She navigated her way through the hardship of cancer treatment, always managing to find balance, always carrying an infectious smile that lit up even the darkest corners of her journey.

Her tenacity was striking. Throughout her battle with cancer, she didn't hold back from expressing her desires or wishes. These were not just demands; they were her hopes, her dreams, and her vibrant spirit dancing amidst the storm.

Our weddings, mine and Priti's, came as a delightful time during this difficult period. Within a year, she had organized beautiful traditional Punjabi wedding ceremonies for us, not allowing her condition to rob her of these joyous and once-in-a-lifetime occasions. As she watched us embark on new journeys, her heart swelled with pride and love, each wedding a testament to her undying spirit.

Her work-related traveling had come to a standstill by her own choice, yet Nikki seized an opportunity to make a trip to the United Kingdom with her family. It was a welcome respite, an intermittent break from chemotherapy to attend a family wedding. She cherished these moments, soaking in the love, warmth, and happiness that flowed freely during such gatherings.

Another joyous time for our family arrived at the birth of Aria, Priti's daughter. Nikki's excitement knew no bounds. The times she spent with Aria were pure bliss. Each time she sang to her, held her little hands, and embraced the baby in her arms, she savored the moments, imprinting them in her heart.

Amidst these celebratory moments, a cloud of sadness descended upon the family. My grandfather, Nikki's father, Dewan Singh, was facing his own health challenges in Yuba City. Their phone conversations, once regular, had dwindled as his health had declined.

One morning, a phone call from my aunt shattered the early morning calm. My grandfather had passed away. A myriad of emotions swelled within me as I made my way to my parents' room. I sat next to my mother, taking her hand in mine, feeling the fragile connection between life and death. I told her about her father's passing. A single tear slid down her cheek, and the only words she said were, "*Okay, let's go.*"

The family came together in Yuba City in mourning and remembrance. We reminisced about our grandfather's life, struggles, successes, strength, and unwavering determination to provide for his family. He was the pillar upon which the family had built their lives, the reason we all were where we were today.

As we bid our final goodbyes to our beloved grandfather, we chose to celebrate his life rather than mourn his loss. We penned down the stories he used to tell us, immortalizing him in words and creating a passage to remember him by. Like Nikki's spirit, his memory was a reminder of the strength inherent in each of us, a testament to the unyielding power of the human spirit.

Chapter 16: Love, Loss, and Legacy

As time mercilessly went past, Nikki began experiencing an unsettling series of symptoms: shortness of breath, discomfort when lying flat, an unusual chest pain, and an incessant feeling of fullness. Fear gnawed at our hearts as we headed back to the oncologist, who ordered a suite of tests, including a PET scan and an echocardiogram.

The diagnosis was like a punch to the gut: malignant pericardial effusion – cancer had invaded the pericardium, leading to fluid accumulation around her heart. But Nikki refused to crumble. She defied the suggestion of hospice or palliative care, believing in her heart that she had a full life ahead of her. Even in the face of such adversity, she declared that she could live another lifetime with these symptoms if it meant continuing the battle.

We returned home after treatment for malignant pericardial effusion, but her health took a nosedive. Every ticking second became a stark reminder that the cancer was getting the best of her, and the treatments were losing their potency.

During this time, I decided to cut back on my work hours, choosing instead to spend every precious moment with Nikki. We had intense, intimate conversations, discussing her desires and wishes for when she would no longer be with us. These were the most emotionally taxing exchanges I had ever had. While the raw honesty and her undying spirit made them precious, the conversations weren't easy.

As the weeks advanced, so did the cancer. The relentless beast introduced a new, distressing symptom - uncontrollable vomiting. My mother couldn't keep anything down, and her strength was beginning to wane. I was constantly worried for her, but I refused to let my concern show, determined to be the rock she needed.

The word 'hospice' took on a haunting tone during those days, lurking ominously at the back of my mind. Our visits to the ER increased. During these, Nikki emphasized her wish to live the remainder of her life with dignity. The light in her eyes never dimmed; her spirit never wavered.

On a particularly luminous July morning that remains vivid in my heart, Nikki, Bentley, and I found ourselves basking in the backyard's warm sunlight. The day held a distinct sense of promise and exhilaration. We had recently imparted to Nikki the delightful news - she was on the cusp of welcoming two more grandchildren, Jaiden and Arian, into her life. Even in her pain, her countenance was a canvas of pure, intense joy. This infectious happiness served as a healing salve, a poignant testament to life's perpetual march, even amidst our shared tribulation.

In spite of her physical discomfort, Nikki desired a simple pleasure − a well-charred hotdog, her favorite, accompanied by a tall glass of buttermilk. We both understood the repercussions that would follow, yet she was prepared to indulge, to take delight in a meal that was close to her heart. In this moment of anticipatory pleasure, we shared a tangible connection, a bond tempered by shared struggles, one that would remain imprinted in our hearts forever.

As I fired up the grill, setting the hot dogs to sizzle and pop, a wave of emotions swept over me. I was preparing what could likely be the last meal I would ever cook for my mother - the woman who taught me to navigate the culinary world and who shared with me her joy and passion for food. Each flip of the hotdog was a stark reminder of the impending reality we were about to face. Yet, there was a bitter-sweet pleasure in doing this for her, in knowing that this simple act was fulfilling one of her wishes.

We ate together, relishing each bite, each moment. The charred taste of the hotdog, the tangy mustard and ketchup, and the cooling buttermilk − it was a strange combination, but it was her choice, her moment. But then, the inevitable followed. The food she had so enjoyed couldn't stay down. She threw it all up. As I held her while she vomited, wiping her clean, she looked at me, and we shared a laugh amidst the tears. It was a moment of powerful connection, a bond forged in shared pain and love.

The subsequent day, from that poignant memory, the decision was reached to transition Nikki into hospice care, but in the familiar setting of our home. We replaced the cold, sterile hospital bed with a cozy one, offering her warmth and comfort. Every morning, we prepared homemade fruit smoothies, hoping to tantalize her fading taste buds, even if for a fleeting moment before nausea would overpower her senses. I swiftly learned the nuances of administering IV fluids to ensure her hydration.

Medications like morphine and fentanyl patches were on hand, ensuring Nikki's comfort was paramount. With spirit, she continued to move, to live every moment until her physical strength began to waver.

Time has a mysterious way of unfolding; at moments, it can seem like an unending river, expanding moments into prolonged stretches, while at others, it swiftly courses forward, turning days into brief instants. In hospice, Nikki's experience was of both. A span of mere days felt like a lifetime, each ticking second brimming with memories, love, and poignant sadness.

When July 13th dawned, darkness hung in the air—that night, marked by its palpable stillness, hinted at a chapter closing. As Nikki's journey on this plane neared its end, the room became a haven of sorrow but also of the love she'd cultivated her entire life.

That evening is forever imprinted in our hearts, a moment suspended in time. As Mom approached her final moments, the weight of our emotions was nearly unbearable. We held her close. The room was filled with the faces of those who loved her, a testament to the life she lived. Amidst the grief, our unity showcased the deep connections she had fostered. As she took her last breath, our tears flowed freely, symbols of our boundless love and loss.

At that moment, she was freed from her burdens, leaving behind a legacy that radiated with undying love, an unyielding spirit, and a luminance that time could never dim.

Chapter 17: A Legacy of Love

I think of her every day. The resilience in her spirit, the strength that never seemed to flicker even in the toughest of times, her journey from a little girl in India to a thriving professional in America, and how beautifully she wore her successes. She was not just my mother; she was my inspiration, my guiding light, my beacon in the storm. Her contagious smile was radiant and genuine, and it became a part of my own identity. It was that smile that connected us all - family, friends, and colleagues alike. And that connection remains, even though she's not physically here anymore.

I feel immensely overwhelmed when I look back and think of everything she has taught me. Nikki was more than a mother; she was a life coach. From her, I learned that strength comes not from circumstances but from within us. I learned the importance of living a life of reason and integrity, of standing firm even when the ground beneath us seems to give way.

Through her journey in hospice, she taught me lessons that no textbook could ever teach. She taught me about the strength in vulnerability, about the beauty in surrender. And most importantly, she taught me about love - selfless, unconditional love transcends even the barriers of life and death.

Nikki believed in spreading love and joy, in living not just for herself but for others, too. Her mission in life wasn't just to survive but to also thrive; and to do so with passion, compassion, humor, and style. She once told me that life is not about creating wealth but about building an empire of love and happiness. An empire where everyone feels valued, loved, and cherished.

I know there is always going to be sorrow in my heart. The hole she has left is immense, a void that can never be filled. But I also know that grief and pain are not the end of my story, nor were they the end of hers.

Through all the pain and sorrow, Nikki found strength. She chose to celebrate life, live fully, and fight bravely. And that is the legacy she has left behind, a legacy of resilience, courage, and boundless love.

I miss my mom so dearly; not a day goes by without her in my thoughts. Each morning I wake up, I carry her in my heart, and with every step I take, I can feel her beside me, guiding me and supporting me. She continues to live in the sound of my laughter, in my joy, and in my strength. She lives in my hopes, my dreams, my aspirations.

Nikki has left an indelible imprint on my life, an imprint of love and strength. I carry her with me, not as a weight that drags me down, but as wings that lift me up, that propel me to move forward, to keep going, no matter how tough things get. And I know as long as I keep her in my heart, she will continue to live on, her legacy will continue to shine, and her love will continue to inspire.

As I pen down these final lines of this book, I want to say - thank you, Mom. Thank you for being you, for showing me the way, for lighting up my life with your love, and for leaving behind a legacy so beautiful, so powerful.

You may have left this world, but you will always be here, in my heart, in my memories, in every sunset and every sunrise, in every smile and every tear. I will always miss you, and I will always love you. But more than anything, I will always remember.